Marriage Matters

Shara Grylls

Pen Press Publishers Ltd

First published in Great Britain by
Pen Press Publishers Ltd
The Old School
39 Chesham Road
Brighton BN2 1NB

ISBN 1-905203-65-9

Illustrations by Charlie Mackesy
Cover design by Jacqueline Abromeit

For Bear,
You are my everything

Foreword

This little book is a compilation of quotes that people gave my husband and I when we got married. We simply asked everyone to enclose with their wedding invitation replies, some words that they thought might help us. We were overwhelmed with great advice.

Some of the quotes are made up and some are classics. There are poems, recipes, sayings, old wives' tales and just simple common sense advice, but overall, the outstanding quality that shines through this book is love. In the good times, in the hard times; love; being a friend when it really matters; protecting each other.

I love being married and I completely adore my husband and therefore this book is for him... with all my love.

Shara Grylls

Acknowledgements

Thank you to all our friends and family who contributed these quotes and sayings, and for making this little book what it is, and finally thank you so much to you, Charlie, for the cartoons, they are like you, inspired.

Shara was born in 1974, is married to Bear Grylls, and is mother to a little boy called Jesse, aged 2. She lives with her family on a Dutch barge on the Thames in London and on a small private Welsh island.

"A good marriage requires you to fall in love many times, always with the same person."

"Do you come here often?"

From Bear's father

"First - Tell each other you love each other
several times each day.
Second - Make each other laugh.
Seeing the funny side of things, and of each other,
is the best 'fuel' for a successful marriage.
Third - Always say to yourself, how will my actions
affect the other.
May God watch over you always."

"Together, live each day like your last and each night, like your first."

"Frequently listen to, appreciate
and touch each other."

"From this day forward,
You shall not walk alone.
My heart will be your shelter,
And my arms will be your home."

"Keep a short account of wrongs."

"Never stop holding hands."

"The giving must always exceed the taking."

"Forget the word 'never'
- you never do this or that."

"There is no more lovely,
friendly and charming relationship,
communion or company
than a good marriage."
- *Oscar Wilde*

"Send her flowers for no reason."

"Couples who pray together stay together."

"Marriage is one plus one equals one."

To the Husband: "Hug and squeeze her daily ... and if her daily won't go along with it, try the au pair!"

"Share baths and alternate who has the taps."

"A house is made of walls and beams; a home is built of love and dreams."

"True love and a hacking cough -
both cannot be hid!"

"Love is like playing the piano.
First you must learn to play by the rules, then you
must forget the rules and play from the heart."

"An archaeologist is the best husband any woman can have: the older she gets, the more interested he is in her."
- *Agatha Christie*

"Do not marry a person that you know you can live with; only marry someone that you cannot live without."

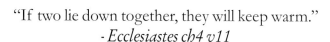

"If two lie down together, they will keep warm."
- *Ecclesiastes ch4 v11*

"Grow old along with me, the best is yet to be."
- *Robert Browning*

"When you're right, be silent and when you're wrong, admit it straight away."

"A successful marriage depends on two things:
(1) finding the right person and
(2) being the right person."

"Be sure to tell one another how much you love each other at every opportunity - or rest assured - someone else will!"

"There are no accidents ... those who are to meet will meet - they are ready for each other."

"Marriage resembles a pair of shears - so joined that they cannot be separated, often moving in opposite directions, yet always punishing anyone who comes between them."
- *Sydney Smith*

"One has not gained a husband,
and the other has not gained a wife,
but both have gained lifelong mates."

"Forget the word 'always' - Why do you *always* forget to order the milk? - Why do you *always* fail to put the seat down?"

"Always retain the ability to laugh at yourself."

"For a good marriage, never lose sight of what brought you both together in the first place."

"Be true to yourself
and you cannot then be false to anyone."

"Enjoy lots of sex."

"Be loyal."

"Be considerate in all things."

"Young lovers seek perfection ... Old lovers seek the art of sewing threads together and seeing beauty in a multiplicity of patches."

"Never sleep on a grievance."

"Lots of weekend breaks."

"Marriage is like life.
What we give out, we get back."

"Don't spend the night in the spare bedroom."

"Now you will feel no rain,
for each of you will be shelter for the other.
Now you will feel no cold,
for each of you will be warmth to the other.
Now there is no more loneliness,
for now you are two persons,
but there is only one life before you.
Go now to your dwelling
to enter into the days of your life together.
And may your days be good
and long upon the earth."
- *Apache Wedding Prayer*

"When asked to do the washing up in the matrimonial home, be sure to drop one or two of the most expensive plates, glasses, bowls. This should ensure that you are never asked for assistance in this area again. Note however, if both parties are using the same tactic, this could be expensive!"

"A honeymoon is the brief period of time between
I do and you'd better!"

"Rule 1. Your wife is always right.
Rule 2. Even when she is wrong, refer to rule 1!"

"Learn to compromise."

"Remember to share the little experiences of every day, so that the times you spend apart can be woven into your times together."

"When two souls, which have sought each other for however long in the throng, have finally found each other, when they have seen that they are matched, are in sympathy and compatible, in a word, that they are alike, there is then established for ever between them a union, fiery and pure as they themselves are, a union which begins on earth and continues for ever in Heaven. This union is love, such as in truth very few men can conceive of that love which is a religion, which defies the loved one, whose life comes from devotion and passion, and for which the greatest sacrifices are the sweetest delights."

- *Victor Hugo*

The Marriage Alphabet

Appreciation

Bewitch

Cherish

Delight

Energise

Forgive

Give

Happiness

Inspire

Joy

Kindness

Love

Multiply

Nurture

Obey

Patience

Question

Resuscitate

Submit

Treasure

Understand

Venerate

Woo

Xpress

Yearn

Zeal

"Be best friends."

"A healthy marriage is like a healthy child - they look up and outward to experience and enjoy all that is good and beautiful and to love and strengthen what is lonely and weak."

"Don't wear anything in bed."

"Get an answering machine."

"Always keep a sense of humour."

"True love protects."

"Listen to each other."

Recipe for a good marriage

Half a cup of friendship and a cup of thoughtfulness.
Creamed together with a pinch of powdered tenderness.
Very lightly beaten in a bowl of loyalty.
With a cup of faith and one of hope and one of charity.
Be sure to add a spoonful each of gaiety that sings,
And also the ability to laugh at little things.
Moisten with the sudden tears of heartfelt sympathy.
Bake in a good natured pan and serve repeatedly.

"When you are apart, ring lots to say how much you love her."
- *Sir John Mills*

"Tying the knot,
As Jagger forgot,
And Henry VIII didn't know,
Keeps things above boards,
Lets the world know you've scored,
A girl that you'll never let go."

"The best marriage is perhaps the one where, under the love of God, each lays their life down for the other."

Law of Love

First, serve your God with heart, mind and strength
And then will grow love for others at length.
Tend it and share it, at first, with each other.
Then let it spill over each neighbour and brother
In Christ, the family, mankind.
Thus, freedom and purpose and blessings
you'll find.
- *The Rev Ken Robinson*

"Marry only for love."

"His owning Oxfordshire has not affected my decision"

"Think of the other person, before yourself."

"As you love each other, grow in the love of God. As you give yourselves to each other, God gives himself to you. As you share your lives together God shares his life with you. As you grow in awareness of each other, grow in awareness of God. Let his love encircle your love, let his love fill your lives. Let him bind you as one together and one with him."

"There is only one happiness in life,
to love and be loved."
- *George Sands*

"Everyday look for some small way to improve your marriage."

"Just once - watch the sunrise together."

"There is no remedy for love than to love more."
- *Henry Thoreau*

"Make your anniversary the most memorable day of the year. Do something out of the ordinary."

"Don't be afraid to show your weakness — vulnerability brings you close."

"If you want to be loved, love and be loveable."
- *Benjamin Franklin*

"It is the little things that make the big difference."

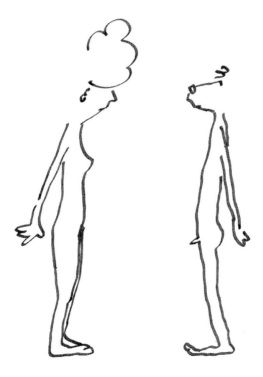

"Don't nag!"

"Leave love notes whenever you go away."

"A successful man is one who can make more money than his wife can spend. A successful woman is one who can find such a man."
- Lana Turner

"If music be the food of love, play on ..."
- *Shakespeare*

"Don't underestimate the power of forgiveness."

"All you need is love."
- *The Beatles*

"Never forget your wedding anniversary."

"Turn off the television at supper time."

"Love is not merely the indulgence of one's
personal tastebuds,
it is also the delight in indulging anothers."
- Laurie Lee

"In the opinion of the world,
marriage ends all, as it does in a comedy.
The truth is precisely the opposite:
It begins all."

"Treasure the love you receive above all.
It will survive long after
your gold and good health have vanished."

"Now you are two persons,
but there is only one life before you."

"Dance together… even in the kitchen
in your pinny!"

"God is always with you, He will always love you,
He will protect you, Bless you and perform
miracles in your life together.
Love Him together."

"I'll love you, Dear, I'll love you,
'til China and Africa meet,
and the river jumps over the mountain,
and the salmon sing in the street.
I'll love you 'til the ocean,
Is folded and hung up to dry,
And the seven stars go squawking,
Like geese about the sky."
- *W.H. Auden*

"Love is like a butterfly.
If you hold it too tightly, you kill it.
If you hold it too lightly, you lose it."

"Don't allow the telephone to interrupt important moments."

"Do not criticise your spouse in front of others."

"One word frees us of all the weight and pain of life; that word is love."
- *Sophacles*

"Don't spread yourselves too thin, learn to say no."

"Put the loo seat down!"

"Never walk out on an argument."

"The need to surrender is one of the great paradoxes of love. Surrender may seem like giving up, or giving in. But in reality we are strengthened when we actively choose to make ourselves vulnerable. We are empowered by sharing our deepest self with another person, offering him or her our heart, our soul, our life. Surrender is an act of free will. A sacred trust."

- Ellen Sue Stern

"Tolerance and wit will make for many happy years shared by two people who love each other."

"The Rabbit and the Rocking Horse"

"How can I become real?"
the little velvet rabbit asked the old rocking horse.
"It's something that happens to you when someone
loves you, for a long time, really loves you."
"Does it hurt?"
"Sometimes," answered the rocking horse,
"but when you are real you don't mind being hurt.
It doesn't happen all at once, you slowly 'Become'.
It takes a long time, and it does not often happen to
people who break easily, or have sharp edges. By the
time you are real your velvet will be worn out and loved
off, And you will look really shabby, but these things
don't matter at all because once you are real you can't be
ugly, except to people who don't know how to love."
- *Margery Williams*

"Love is the joy of the good, the wonder of the wise, the amazement of the Gods."
- *Plato*

"Be to her virtues very kind.
Be to her faults a little blind."

"Keep one night a week special,
for just the two of you."

"Look round our world; behold the chain of love
Combining all below and all above."
- *Alexander Pope*

"There is no greater happiness than that of sharing life with all its joys and cares as a husband and wife."

"Help with the ironing,
even if you make a mess of it."

"Say Grace at meal times."

"Compliment each other daily."

"Marriage is like glass. The more you work at it - the more precious it becomes."

"Love does not consist of gazing at each other but in looking together in the same direction."
- *Antoine de Saint-Exupery*

"Marriage is like two stones becoming one by grinding together, the hard bits of one wearing away the soft bit of the other, until at last the fit is perfect; one stone."
- *Sheldon Vanauken*

"Fetch each other a cup of water in the night."

"If the grass is greener on the other side of the hill
... it's time to start watering your own!"